How To Gain
Real Financial
Independence

PO Box 3464
Dural NSW 2158
AUSTRALIA

ISBN: 1-4392-1453-0
ISBN-13: 9781439214534

To order additional copies, visit
www. drjamesellingford.com
www.booksurge.com
www.amazon.com
or your local book store

How To Gain Real Financial Independence

The Seven Golden Rules To Wealth

Dr James Ellingford

About the Author

James Ellingford happily retired at the age of 42 with the time he needs to do what he wants to do and when he wants to do it. He retired so that he could pursue his dream of helping others, educate the public in relation to investments and perhaps, more importantly, to spend more time with his family and friends.

James Ellingford's professional life culminated in being head of a billion dollar business based in Geneva, Switzerland. It was during this time that James learnt again, first hand, the lessons that would prove so useful in focusing his attention, time and effort for what was to come.

James Ellingford's hard hitting, straight to the point management style not only earned him respect and trust from his peers but also undoubtedly caused its usual share of upsets along the way.

He holds a Post Graduate in Corporate Management, Masters in Business Administration as well as a Doctorate in Management. He is not only more than qualified to discuss the theory and practice surrounding investments but also more than capable of delivering the information in a provocative, direct and albeit sometimes controversial manner - to enable those of us with even little or no knowledge of the stock market - to be able to take control of our own financial future - and succeed! Love him or hate him, one thing is for sure, you won't forget what he has to say.

Special Thanks

There are a few people whom I would like to thank, for without their support this book would not have been possible.

Firstly, I would like to thank someone who gave freely of his time and asked for nothing in return. Peter Thornhill is that person for me, that one special person who was able to succinctly articulate what I thought I knew and more importantly gave me the confidence to act. Thank you, Peter.

I also want to thank my wife Claire who provided encouragement at every turn. She has shown me total trust and kindness throughout our journey together and I am blessed to have found such a wonderful human being. Thank you.

Without these two very special people none of this would have been possible.

Table of Contents

Foreword

In my late teens, I started to question more and more the concepts of time, money and the different investment options which were available. Over that time I became more and more frustrated by the lack of clarity, truthfulness and sometimes outright morally incomprehensible behaviour of the financial and investment markets. As such, I have written this book so that you can gain a clear understanding of how things really are.

Over the past years I have been fortunate enough to help many people learn the value of time and what time can create in terms of one's own financial security. I have also spent much of my time recanting the same stories time and time again to people who genuinely seemed interested in listening and who always came back and asked for more.

Over the past few years, in particular, I have been continually encouraged to write down what I know and it is for this reason that I wrote this book. I hope that this book acts as a conduit by providing a wider audience with some of the missing pieces.

My hope is, that in the years to come there is far more financial education available to a much wider audience and that this education is delivered in a far more holistic approach rather than the traditional asset versus liability model that simply misses the point. Financial goals are simply one small part of the overall picture and by ignoring the balance i.e. the person, their hopes, dreams and ambitions for the future, is to miss the point altogether.

Background

I am not interested in writing yet another mellow book on 'how to' without providing a clear framework of how to achieve your goals. I am also going to make the consequences for inaction crystal clear. Often people recant what others have said in a way that is supposed to make the speaker sound more intelligent than they really are. People repeat stories in a way that makes the receiver believe that the message is one hundred percent fact. People in general have a fundamental flaw of believing what others say rather than doing the hard yards to find out what the facts really are. Get the facts and get ahead as substance is what counts in the long run. Let the general population believe what they want just don't follow blindly. Trust me, you will be better off.

I believe it is critically important to say from the get go that I am not the cleverest and certainly would never want to mislead anyone into believing that what I had to say was anything more than comment. That being said, I did retire early (FACT), I did run a billion dollar business (FACT) I do have a Doctorate (FACT) and I am very happy (FACT) so while I may not be the sharpest tool in the shed, I am sharp enough.

I believe that if you are going to read this book you should know a little about me, and what influences shaped my life as this is important in how my theories and thoughts solidified into what they are today.

Finally, I promise to write this book in a way that even a person with no understanding of financial markets or goal setting will understand.

My Early Years

I recall seeing my mother return home from a parent teacher night with tears running down her face telling my father that my grade five primary school teacher, Mrs Champ had told her, "I suppose we need someone to dig drains – your son is simply not cut out for school". While this overheard news was somewhat devastating it did, however, provide me with a raison d'etre, to prove my worth to the world. The reason I recall this story and refer to it now fondly, is that this was the catalyst for providing me with the drive to achieve beyond all expectations and was the spark that in some way lit the fire in my belly to succeed. So Mrs Champ wherever you are, I thank you.

Success then to an eleven year old was having enough money to buy an ice cream, Rubik's cube, yo-yo or whatever was the latest craze at that time – a symbol of one's worth that was easily recognized by my peers. I soon realised that money brought with it the power to purchase items that others envied and that with material objects I could escalate my position within the eyes of others and, as such, increase my feeling of social worth and acceptance among my peers.

As a young adult I could not wait to leave school to earn money as I then thought that the power and freedom money bought was worth more than any academic achievement. It is not as if you wore your leaving school certificate around your neck like a badge of honour. No one knew if you were academically gifted or not but society viewed those who drove a smart car, wore nice clothes, had cash in their pockets as being successful. It was these experiences that led me to the clear conclusion that if I worked hard I could have all the things others envied and that this, in some way, would make me feel whole.

My Twenties

Through my twenties my hard work paid off, being promoted through various organisations from junior to mid level management positions until I was headhunted by a large Singaporean company who offered me the ultimate role – Divisional General Manager, Third Party Products. I was made! In actual fact, it was this role that led to my ultimate downfall and which has provided me with valuable life lessons for which I am incredibly grateful.

During my years with the Singaporean company I was married, had two wonderful children, matching BMWs, a house in the right area, a cruiser moored at a rather up-market marina and a gold watch to signal to all that cared that I was a success. Money was not an issue and life, as far as I could tell, was going to plan. I was convinced that I had the Midas touch and that nothing could hurt me as long as I worked hard, did the right thing and continued to focus on making money.

With money and a severe lack of maturity came a disgraceful attitude that I was superior to all others and that unless another person had the boat, flash cars and a smart house they were worthless and beneath my position in life. As such, I would rarely consider acknowledging the existence of others! I really was an arrogant twat!

I was in my mid twenties, materially successful and was disliked by my family, friends and just about all whom I came in contact with. This dislike people had of me I vainly put down to jealousy on their part and the Australian "tall poppy" syndrome. I was so consumed by money, conversations about money and only being interested in what things cost that I never spent time to appreciate the real value of things *(read that sentence again)*.

By my late twenties I had offended everyone I had ever been in contact with including and for the last time my then wife, whom on return from a business trip, I found had left, taking our two children. How could this be? I was successful, had the Midas touch, the cars, the house, the boat. How could it be that my wife could hate me so much as to leave the family home? The answer that soon became apparent was that success and money had absolutely nothing to do with each other.

Over the next few months I left my job, lost my cars, house and boat and turned to the only thing that made me feel and helped me forget; alcohol. It was during this time that I met my present wife who wasn't interested in cars, boats, or where I lived, had no interest in money or my current bank balance (or lack of it) and who was more interested in experiencing life, helping others and being true to one's self.

Changing Values

During my thirties I took up a post with a technology company in Japan and moved to Tokyo to help rebuild my life, save some money and take the only job that was on offer. The realization that one's life could be so satisfying without the trappings of money was to become incredibly obvious. Living in a typical Japanese style apartment no larger than the laundry in my previous home, feeling satisfied with life and completely happy made me understand for the very first time that money was a by-product of one's work and had no relationship to happiness or success.

On returning to Australia after spending two years in Japan I was no more the arrogant, self serving individual that I had been before but rather a more tolerant and socially minded person that truly believed I had no more the right to judge others as others had to judge me.

The next decade saw me develop into a far more humble and accepting person as my career flourished yet again. After another stint overseas – this time in England and Switzerland, I have remembered the lessons life has taught me which has enabled me to be truly successful both professionally and personally.

The main reason I do what I do in three words is – to help others. The reason I want to help others is so that I can give back to others my experience of life in the hope that it adds value to theirs. Giving back to others, helping others, coaching others, seeing others develop both professionally and personally is far more satisfying than any bonus cheque from head office, far more fulfilling than allowing others to judge you via society's material symbols of wealth and far more worthwhile than any material item that can be bought.

Those whom judge others via material objects are themselves shallow, empty little people who are no doubt unhappy with their lot in life. I truly feel sorry for these people who can be our neighbours, relatives and even sometimes our friends. Do not judge them but rather understand that these people are helping us build our wealth! Yes! Their insatiable appetite for the latest gadget, the best shoes, the latest handbag or the newest car is what drives our wealth.` Clearly they need to get a grip on what is important in life but sadly they lack the internal fortitude to break free from the shackles of the material world preferring instead to be part of the pack. Read on and you will see.

The Stories That Stick

There are two stories I was told long ago that have helped guide me through life's trappings. I believe that these two stories encapsulate everything there is, in simple digestible, manageable pieces so that no matter where you are in life these stories can be used to guide and support your ambitions and goals so that they can become a reality.

Those with whom I have worked over the years would be very familiar with me recanting these stories as it is these stories that I used and continue to use to this day to help explain just about every step I take. If we were to implement a major project in Switzerland, Germany, France, Spain, or in any region we would always break it down into manageable parts. Companies do not implement major projects without a thorough plan so why is it that we believe that we can go through life without one. Simply put, you can't.

The following two stories sum up far more eloquently than I can how to achieve goals beyond your wildest dreams.

The River

Something that I was told long ago which remains true to this day is that life is a little like a river flowing downstream. If you try to get to the other side by jumping in, the water will swallow you up and dump you a long way from where you intended to be. If, however, you throw a rope over to the other side, anchor it and jump in, the stream will still tug at you and try and pull you off course but by maintaining focus on the rope and pulling yourself through the water you will find, in time, that you will end up exactly where you intended. After all if you don't know where you're going you may end up someplace else. Someplace else that is nearly always far less satisfying than one would have hoped for.

The above story which I have often repeated has been slightly modified over the years. The rope has now been replaced by stepping stones, with each stepping stone representing a three year span of life. I know that so long as I complete all the objectives connected to each stepping stone then by the time I get to the other side I will be exactly where I intended to be. I truly believe that as people we need to have discipline and learn the art of planning if we are to truly add value to our lives, meet our goals and be there for those around us, as they will be there for us.

Many, many years ago I fondly recall entering my marketing director's office and I asked him, "Why do you have a picture of a car on your wall?" Well, he said with a certain satisfaction, "that is to remind me of one of my goals". He then went onto remind me of a conversation we both had where I had recanted the river story. Not only had he listened but he had acted. I left the office that day realizing that someone's life had been changed in a positive way from this story. For the record he ended up getting his dream car a few years later and while I would have preferred he bought shares he certainly now realizes the power of planning.

I personally find it very frustrating that the financial organisations that exist in this country and for that matter around the world only ever talk about having a financial plan and to hell with the rest. It is all well and good having a financial plan but without a life plan it could all be for nothing. No point in saving hard if you are to end up in the divorce courts or worse still, stuck in an unhappy marriage. No point being worth a few million dollars if at retirement you find that your partner has other ambitions and ideas on how to spend the money. No point having a million dollars if in retirement what you need is ten. Without a totally planned approach to life none of us have any real chance of success.

The other story I often recant is what I refer to as the Daffodil Principle. I do love this story as it clearly demonstrates a number of very important things.

The Daffodil Principle

Several times a friend had telephoned to say, "You must come see the daffodils before they are over." I wanted to go, but it was always never a good time to make the trip to see, what I was lead to believe, was an amazing show of daffodils and by the time I did the daffodil show was over. Driving back home, however, I noticed a sign on the road saying "Daffodils This Way". So I turned the corner only to come across the most amazing five acres of daffodils. But who has done this? Leading up the road through the daffodils was a sign that simply read, "Answers to All Your Questions".

The first answer;

"50,000 bulbs"

The second;

"One at a time"

The third.

"Began in 1958"

Here it was, The Daffodil Principle! For me, that moment was a life-changing experience.

I thought of this person whom I had never met, who, more than forty years before, had begun - one bulb at a time - to bring his/her vision of beauty and joy to an obscure mountain top. Still, just planting one bulb at a time, year after year, had changed the world and created something of magnificence, beauty, and inspiration.

The principle that daffodil garden taught is one of the greatest principles of life. That is, learning to move towards our goals and desires one step at a time, often one baby-step at a time, learning to love the doing and learning to use the accumulation of time to our advantage is the greatest gift of all. Simply put, when we multiply tiny pieces of time with small increments of daily effort, we too will find we can accomplish magnificent things.

So, stop waiting until your car or home is paid off. Until you get a new car or home. Until your kids leave the house. Until you go back to school. Until you finish school. Until you lose 10kgs. Until you gain 10kgs. Until you get married. Until you get a divorce. Until you have kids. Until you retire. Until summer, spring, winter or autumn. There is no better time than right now to be happy and financially secure. Happiness is a journey, not a destination. So work like you don't need money. Love like you've never been hurt and dance like no one's watching as life is now and let me assure you, life is not a dress rehearsal.

In both of the above stories there is one common theme: plan and you will succeed, fail to plan and you will not. Life is just like this and as it is your life then it's time to start planning as without a plan, a course, a direction one becomes a little like a ship without a rudder, without control and without any hope of arriving at your chosen destination. Without taking responsibility for your own life and its directions what hope do you have of achieving your goals? How do you know when your goals have been achieved? Without a plan what is the point of everything?

Do not hold governments responsible for your situation. Don't hold business to task because of the increase in the cost of basic necessities and, finally, do not accept everything you hear or read to be without bias. People need to take responsibility for their own future and this book will give you the tools so that you can reach your wildest dreams regardless of the country, jurisdiction or economic climate you are in. That said, have no doubt that planning will require daily effort and goal setting but if you follow this through I promise that you will have the power to make the impossible, possible.

Planning: The Key To Everything

What never ceases to amaze me is the lack of any real planning people do in their lives. Sure, most have some vague ideas about what they want and how they think they are going to get there but as for concrete, defined, written plans then forget it. Is it any wonder then why we are a nation of people who have no idea of where we are going and a nation of people who live for the moment devouring more and more debt? Is this the reason why we are a nation of people who are happy to accept whatever we are told or could it be the reason why there are so many grumpy old (retired) men in this country of ours?

In any case the reality is that without some basic written goals, without a structure and well thought through plan and without the commitment to creating one you've either just wasted your money by buying this book and your life will be less than perfect and full of regrets or you are about to take a most fascinating journey of discovery that will deliver exactly what you plan for. Sir William Olser once said, "We are here to add what we can to, not get what we can from, life" (Walsh, 2004).

A few years ago I was in London at a function with my peers when an elderly gentleman introduced himself to me and said, "Hello, my name is James Toltington I used to be a senior tax consultant". This, for some unknown reason bothered me immensely at the time but it was not until recently that I discovered that nine times out of ten when I am introduced to someone that the person's name and/or position is listed as a way of identifying that person's pecking order in life. Surely there is more to life than this? Surely these retired men have more to offer than listing their past achievements as a way of justifying their existence? Surely men generally have more to offer the nation than their rank and file, if not, then not only do I feel sorry for them but I feel incredibly sorry for their wives.

This system of human introduction started to grate on my conscious thought and, as such, made me realise that I wanted and needed to avoid at all costs any association with my position in life, when in retirement. I am constantly amazed at how many seemingly highly accomplished retired executives I meet introduce themselves in such a manner. I'm an ex bank manager or I'm an ex CEO. Is this the reason that there are so many grumpy old men in society? Has their reason for living been removed in retirement?

Have all these grumpy old men sold their soul in some way to the trappings of the corporate world? Are they simply empty shells without any purpose? Is this the reason they struggle in later years when the corporate world discards them for the newer, younger, smarter and more improved model of man?

Countless books are available for one to read on how to become successful according to the material, western societal definition of the word but what I want to know is where are the books on retiring happy?

In a US best seller, "How to Become CEO", the author writes about one's family in a way that is totally devoid of reality. "Put family activities on the to do list, respond to your family in the same manner you respond to a big client", and "Support your family, it will help your career" (Fox, 2000). Is this author living in the real world? Do we really need to read and learn about using our family in order to gain the next position on the corporate ladder and is this really what life is meant to be with the job coming before family? I learnt it was the other way around.

To be avoided at all costs, however, is the seemingly inevitable conclusion of one's later years becoming tired, boring and grumpy. While I appreciate and understand how retired men reach the point of frustration I also realise that this is not what I wish for myself, my wife or my family. To have dreams, to fulfill ambitions and to contribute to society is the real measure of success and to have half a chance of making this a reality one must plan.

"Jeanne Calment, believed to be the world's oldest person, died at age 122, but at the age of 85, she took up fencing lessons and at 100 years of age, she was still riding a bicycle" (CNN, 2004). "It is said today it is conceivable that people in there [sic] 30's may indeed live until 120 years of age" (WOW, 2004). Perhaps it's now time to start planning what we really want from life as there will be so much more of it to enjoy or more to simply survive, if like most, you have no plan.

During my life I have been fortunate to meet and spend time with people who have the courage of their convictions and do not accept the normal western experience of life as the way one should behave or live. It is this experience together with a combination of events that has allowed me to gain a clear understanding of how to be truly successful.

Success is not found in the corporate boardroom, manipulating the truth, colouring the facts. This is not success, never was and never will be. Success is not driving a flash car or wearing a nice watch. Success is not the latest handbag or shoes and success is not what marketers of this world would have you believe. Success is having the freedom, the real freedom of choice and the time you need to enjoy it.

The time to act is now. Everyone can achieve just about anything they set their minds to so long as one remains committed, passionate, focused and above all else honest with one's own self and those around them.

How To Create
The Life Plan

While the title of this book is "How to Invest to Gain Real Financial Independence" it is simply not possible to do this without having a life plan. Don't be tempted to circumnavigate this process or not allow yourself the time to fully explore and understand this concept as without a life plan you will not succeed. Trust me, everyone who is a success by whatever definition you wish to give that word, has a life plan in one form or another.

The life plan should be viewed as the foundation stone for the rest of your life. It is the stone from which everything is built. It is the stone that will support your ambitions, dreams and hopes for the future and it is the stone that holds together the mortar of life and with it, your future. To not cherish this stone (life plan), understand it fully or try in any way to short circuit it, will bring with it the inevitable collapse dragging down you, your family, your friends and your dreams with it. Your life plan (foundation stone) is the point where everything comes together in a meaningful way and is the light that will guide you through life's challenges along the way.

In the river story I talked about a rope across a stream. This rope is basically your life plan. I also talked about stepping stones filled with objectives, dreams, moments, mile-stones; this is also your life plan. The Daffodil Principle talked of allowing time to create your dream, vision, hopes and ambitions; this is your life plan. The Daffodil Principle also spoke of taking one step at a time; this too is your life plan. To put no finer point on it your life plan is your reason for being and it is your ticket to create the most fulfilling life possible which includes having the financial freedom of choice. There is no greater gift than the gift real financial freedom brings.

So how does one create a life plan? With a lot of soul searching. Your life plan must be a written document that you either do on your own if you are single or together with your partner if you are married or in a long term relationship. After all you are in partnership with another human being and, as such, taking for granted that he/she will accept your life plan/direction would be a huge mistake. People can have different dreams and ambitions from those of their partner, so long as everyone is on the same page and that both parties understand what the other wants, it is generally not a problem. Problems occur when your partner does not know.

The first step in the process of creating a life plan is to ask yourself a series of, on the surface, seemingly simple questions:

- Where do I/we want to be in two years?
- Where do I/we want to live?
- Where do I/we want to retire?
- How much money do I/we really need?
- What do I/we really want to do?
- When do I/we want to retire?
- Where do I/we want to be in five, ten, fifteen, twenty years?
- What will I/we do when I/we retire?
- Where will I/we live when I/we retire?

These questions, when you really start thinking about them, are far harder than they actually appear to be on the surface. They require clarity of thought and commitment on your part to extract the truth for without truth there is no point in continuing. To drive a leased BMW pretending you can afford it is ridiculous. You can have a million dollars, a BMW and a boat but what you need is a fulfilling life and in order to achieve this you need to understand what it is that you really want as you may be surprised to learn that it wasn't the big house, the flash car or the fancy boat that you wanted/needed after all.

Time and time again, friends of mine come and show me their life plans. Often these plans clearly show a couple going in different directions. Recently, close friends of my wife and I started to write down their goals and ambitions and within minutes of reviewing their plans with them it was clear that they were going in completely opposite directions. The wife wanted to travel with work and gain a posting to the USA, while the husband was happy to continue running his own (successful) business. When I pointed the problem out the wife shocked us all and said simply, "I could leave for a few years and come back". Needless to say this was not what the husband had in mind. While I am not a trained counselor I could see there were issues that needed to be resolved, as such, I suggested that the couple seek professional help. The process of going through their journey proved that if there were much more planning going on in marriages and more honest, direct communication then there would be far fewer divorces. I am pleased to say that the couple remain married and are happily pursuing their life dreams after much thought, consideration and communication.

The reality is that if two people have grown apart then that's perfectly acceptable, leave and move on. What is not acceptable is not knowing what you or your partner wants or where you and your partner are headed. There is no point in kidding yourself or others that you are happy, that your life is fulfilled when it is not, as time has a wonderful way of digging in and exposing the truth. We all need to stop from time to time and re-test our own assumptions about life and the relationships we have rather than bury our head in the sand and acquire yet more material possessions.

I can't stress the importance of creating a life plan but I can tell you that once you have done this the rest is easy. The finances, the goals, the dreams will all fall into place and make complete sense but first you and your partner need to sit down and work through what it is that you want from life as without clear goals and direction you will not succeed.

During my time running a large company many of my senior directors felt that if only they earned a bit more life would be easier. Now, these guys were already earning very good incomes so it was hard to believe that they would require more! The point is the more they earned the more they wanted. The more toys, houses, cars they owned and slowly but surely the more in debt, the more disillusioned and unhappy they became. I know it is hard to believe but it is true. Money and happiness have nothing to do with each other.

There was one very senior colleague who asked me one day why was it that I didn't drive a new car, wore an old watch and why it was that I didn't have all the trappings and toys that everyone else did? The reason, I said quite simply, was because I had a plan. Slowly but surely he continued to probe further and over the course of the next few months I had shared with him what I was doing with my life, my investment philosophies and in turn clarified for him my understanding of what was important in life and how to create a life plan.

His initial reaction was surprise but within the following three months he had sold his flash car, sold his house in London, stopped buying Ralph

Lauren shirts and Hugo Boss suits and started to enjoy the freedom from debt and the income from his investments. I am pleased to report that to this day he remains focused on his family and building long term wealth that will provide him with income for the rest of his life.

The point is, sometimes you may think you are doing the right thing as mostly everyone around you is doing it too but it is not until further investigation that you realise that what's important are not the material objects in our lives but the personal contact we have with people we meet throughout our life. One thing is for sure; on our death beds none of us will be saying I wish I had another five million in the bank. We will, however, wish we had more time to spend with those we love.

Sobering thoughts indeed, but as I said, life is not a dress rehearsal but rather a journey we travel. The question is, do you want to be in the driver's seat and arrive at your destination as planned or would you prefer to sit in the back of the bus and see where life drops you off? If you are like me then hopefully the latter will not appeal and you will start taking action in creating your life plan without delay.

It is critically important that your life plan be measurable in every respect and my advice to make things easier is to start at the end first and work your way back. The reason you start at the end is that you may in fact want to retire to Fiji and help villages in remote areas. If this is the case then your financial requirements to support this life choice would be considerably less than if you wanted to retire, maintain your existing house and travel to Europe for six months of the year. During this process you must analyse and understand what and where you want to be so that you can understand what you will require financially to support that lifestyle choice.

To give you an idea of how you should approach this let us start with the last suggested question (above) first. Where will I/we live when I/we retire? The quick answer would be to say Sydney, London, New York or Timbuktu but what is required is much greater thought. What you need to do is imagine yourself in the future living somewhere. What does it look like? Where is it? How big or small is the house? Is it a house or an apartment? Is it near the beach or in land? Is it in Australia, America or Europe? Where? What colour roof tiles does it have? Do you have neighbours? If so how many and who are they?

Ok, so maybe this is too much but it is an example to help you understand how many sub questions there are to each question that you will need to dig into to get to the real truth.

The answer to this question may look something like this;

Q. Where will I/we live when I/we retire?

A. I will retire to my own two bedroom apartment, within three kms of the Sydney GPO. I will live there from the age of 65 until I can no longer manage independent living. I want to live in a building that predominately has professional tenants and or owners and ideally it should be located on George Street, Sydney.

As you can see from this answer there is lot of detail about where this person wants to live when they retire. This detail is critical in creating a proper life plan and for the life plan to work it must have this level of detail. As you go through your life plan you may in fact change your mind as other choices become more important. The only way to know for sure what the outcome will be is to sit down and work though the process. The amount of effort you put into your plan will be directly rewarded in the years to come.

To continue with another example to help you on your journey, let us look at another question. What will I/we do when I/we retire? This is a classic question and I promise you that if you were to ask most men this question the responses often given would be monosyllabic at best. If on the other hand you were to ask a woman this question you would get a cohesive well thought through answer. The fact that men in the main make most of the financial investment decisions should be enough to scare all women half to death! Since my retirement there is no doubt that one thing has become increasingly obvious: that most women are underrated, undervalued and underpaid! God help the women of this world, I say, and more power to them!

However, I digress. Back to the question. The goal here is that you must be able to precisely answer what it is that you want to do in retirement. You must be able to allow yourself the freedom to dream and visualize what it really is that you want. If you want to bungee jump naked from Niagara Falls then write it down. If you want to teach English to children from poor socio-economic South American towns then say so. The only prerequisite is that you are brutally honest with yourself.

Again, an answer to this particular question may look like this;

Q. What will I/we do when I/we retire?

A. When I retire I want to learn how to speak French. I want to have at least one lesson per week. I want to also play 18 holes of golf one day per week preferably on a Monday starting at 9:00am at my local club. I also want to travel to Europe at least every other year for a period of six weeks to visit my family and friends in both England and France. I also want to volunteer at the ....

You can clearly see from these two examples that the level of detail required is onerous and that you must commit the necessary time and effort so that you too can extract what is really important.

As you go through this process you will find the things you thought you wanted you no longer want and things you never considered becoming more important. You may find your partner wants no part of your dream to bungee jump naked from Niagara Falls but interestingly books your flight quickly online (telling!). The reality is that your life plan needs to become your foundation stone and needs to be something you refer to often, refresh annually to check its validity, change when required and something that is pure truth. If you can achieve this then everything else becomes incredibly easy.

I spoke earlier about a colleague of mine who wanted to know why it was that I didn't have a flash car, or flash watch and the reason for this was simple, and that is it would take me longer to achieve my goals. I vividly remember driving in Geneva, Switzerland one day with my wife and children after spending a lovely day having lunch in the French Alps when all of a sudden we drove past Ferrari, Geneva HQ.

Beautiful red, black and silver Ferraris to the right, centre and left, beckoning all who passed as they twinkled in the window. We could have turned the car around in that split instance and bought one. Instead we looked at each other and instantly knew that would be the wrong choice as it was not part of our life plan. This is the internal strength required if you truly want to have the choice and freedom to choose. That's the power of a life plan.

Dreams are free and dreams are often far more satisfying than the real thing so dream all you like but whatever you do, understand the real cost of owning some of these toys that life throws in front of you. I promise you that the actual dream is far more satisfying than ownership could ever be.

Once you have competed your life plan, which may take a few weeks to do properly you will then be able to look at all things far more clearly than before. You will know and for some of you for the first time in your lives, what direction you are headed and how you intend to get there. Remember small stepping stones across a river, small daily effort and I promise time will take care of the rest.

Everything you are, everything you believe, everything you want to achieve needs to be encapsulated in your two, maximum three page life plan. Once completed you will then realise how much money is required to fund your retirement dreams and for most it will be a shock. Do not panic at this stage. Remember the Daffodil Principle will take effect and do what it has always done, weaving the magic of time with your plan to help create great things and make the impossible, possible.

It is an amazing feeling to see for the first time where you are headed and how you are going to get there. I am not saying life will not throw the odd curve ball your way but with you and your plan in hand there is nothing that can push you off course, a little like the rope across the stream of life. So long as you hold onto your dreams, remain focused and committed to achieving your objectives, then in time, you will end up exactly where you want to be.

As the creation of a life plan is so crucial in creating financial independence I have made available a life plan template for those requiring more help with the process. This is available from www. drjamesellingford.com.

From Life Plan To Finance

So you are now ready to invest in you and your life but don't know where to start. Not sure if what you are being told is right or wrong? Feel confused and stressed by it all that it feels easier just to do nothing at all? Trust me when I say you have done the hard work already by doing your life plan, the rest from here is easy, really easy and even if you make the odd mistake along the way the Daffodil Principle will soon correct it.

The following sections will break investing down into manageable pieces so that you will be able to understand the core concepts surrounding money, investment, growth, income and tax. **I will tell you what financial institutions won't.**

The objective is that once you have read this that you have a very real understanding of the concepts surrounding investments and how these concepts all hang together but more importantly how they are inextricably linked to your life plan.

Money for money's sake is repulsive and of no interest to me. I could not seriously care less if you have ten dollars, one million or one hundred million dollars as it is simply not relevant. What is relevant is making sure you have enough income to support your life choices so that you can do what you want in your life rather than what you have to. Once you have the power of choice, real choice that is, you will soon understand that there is no greater gift.

Following, I will discuss the concepts of:

- The share market.
- Investment time horizon.
- The importance of two dimensional assets.
- The real difference between assets and liabilities.

Without wanting to repeat myself all of the following information will be irrelevant and you will not succeed if you fail to have an honest life plan in place. There is no way around doing the plan if you want to succeed. For the last time your financial goals and dreams are intrinsically linked to your life and, as such, if you have no life plan in place you will fail. Living without a plan is like flying a jumbo jet blind. Living without a life plan is like trying to turn a cargo ship without a rudder. The bottom line is that it is not going to work. If you want proof, look around you.

I grew up in a loving family with traditional parents and am the youngest of three. My father was the kind of person who, without fail, arrived ten minutes before he was due for appointments and a person who felt a certain pleasure in paying tax rather than being owed a refund. My father was a man who lived by incredibly high standards which in some areas I have been fortunate enough to inherit. However, when it came to money, my father was, to be blunt, clueless. Like most people my father cared more about the cricket scores than how his superannuation was performing.

He preferred term deposits, he dithered for eleven years on where his superannuation funds should be placed while they sat in a non interest bearing account and while he was a highly intelligent fully functioning member of society he lacked any real foresight, forethought or interest when it came to money.

That's fine, if you, like my father, don't care, lack interest in money, lack the motivation to find out all you can about it, close this book now and throw it in the bin and prepare for a miserable existence in the later years of your life. There is nothing surer. Your miserable years, I might add, are fast approaching and will last much longer than you think.

The reality is that all too often people simply do not care until it is too late. What I am asking for is a little bit of effort daily to help your daffodils grow. The health of your daffodils needs to become the single most important thing in your life because if they die, so do your dreams. I realise that this is harsh and may be upsetting but it is life and correct me if I am wrong but I didn't see any charity sign on the door of life when I entered. Life is hard and sometimes it requires effort so while the concepts of money may not be familiar and may go against what you believe in please hang in there as your time and effort will be rewarded. Of that, I have no doubt.

The outcome is guaranteed for those of you who plan their lives and focus the necessary amount of energy day in and day out, while those who don't, won't.

The Share Market

The day I saw the performance of the Australian Share Market (Figure #1) for the last one hundred years graphically represented was the day that it all started to slowly make sense. I might add that this could also be the American Share Market, the London Share Market, the Swiss Share Market or just about any of the major world markets. This was also the day that led to a meeting with a man who encapsulated and verbalised what I thought I knew, in such a way that made everything crystal clear. This person was able to encourage me to have enough confidence to trust the market to do what it had always done which was, perform.

The Australian share market (could be any major market) is the most wonderfully secure, wonderfully reliable and wonderfully stable mechanism for transferring real wealth to those with the strength of character and patience required to see it through. I am not about buying and selling shares, pushing the razzle dazzle of the markets or having my picture taken sitting in front of the latest Ferrari saying look at me world, how clever am I? There are plenty of these morons making fools of themselves far better than I ever dare. Don't be fooled by those claiming to be able to make a quick buck as it will end up in tears. It always has and always will.

I implore you to not view figure #1 from right to left but rather from right to right. Imagine what the next 100 years will bring? Wow, that makes everything very cheap all of a sudden. The greatest problem mankind has had to endure is that of perception. My perception is my reality and I am very glad I view the world the way I do. What about you?

When I speak of investing I speak of buying shares in quality companies for at the very least a thirty year time horizon. I simply mean that when I buy shares I basically plan to never, ever, ever sell the holdings that I buy. I promise you that this is the only way to approach the markets, has always been the only way to approach the markets and will continue to be the only way to approach the markets. Those who sell leave behind great wealth, nothing surer.

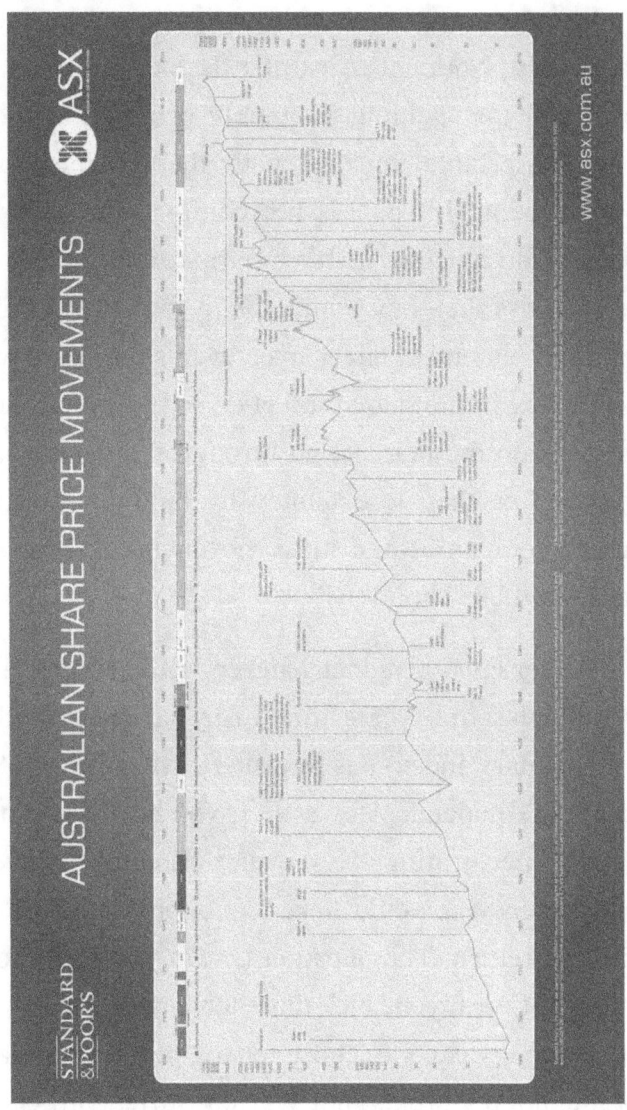

Figure #1. (ASX, 2008)

When you are faced with buying into a business, let us say National Australia Bank and plan to never sell that holding it quickly brings into focus how comfortable you are with that business and your decision. If you are not comfortable with the business do not buy it. If you are comfortable with the business then buy it and hold it for at least thirty years and remember never, ever, ever, sell. Those who lose money in the share market do so by crystallizing losses when the markets go through their inevitable gyrations or they lose money by buying less than quality companies and make no mistake, there are plenty of those about.

The reason I personally never sell is simply this; over the last ten years the Australia share market (All Ordinary Index) has returned a staggering 258% including dividends. However, if you had missed the best ten performing days over that same ten year period then you would have lost approximately one third the return. The question is, can you pick those ten days? Can anyone pick those ten days? The answer is no. Nobody can pick those ten top performing days not me, not my broker, not Warren Buffet, Bill Gates or for that matter not my four year old daughter. In actual fact she has as much chance of getting it right as Warren Buffet, so that basically says it all. The only way you can benefit from the astonishingly secure, safe and predictable wealth creation device, the share market, with certainty is to buy quality companies and never sell. That's it. Not hard, no science, no tricks, no razzle dazzle, no flash cars, no flash presentations, nothing but simple truth, simple fact and simple to follow advice.

I have spoken about buying into quality companies and you are probably saying sure, great, how do we know what is a quality company? Don't worry I will address this later in the book.

Let me state from the outset that I could write an entire book on the amazing, predictable, reliable, stable, safe performance of the Australian share market or just about any other major global market but I won't as that is not the title of this book nor for that matter where my interest lies but simply put, if you had $100.00 dollars and had invested it in the Australian share market in 1900 it would be worth $59,036 today. However, if you had also reinvested the dividends during the same period your investment would be now worth $7,197,512. That means your investment would have grown 71,975 times during the last 106 years.

$7,197,512 is what you would have. No tricks, no razzle dazzle, no Ferraris, no flash in the pan, no fees, no nothing. Simply put you would have $7,197,512 in your hot little hands. Now it is critically important to note that this amazing performance was during the last 106 years during which time we have seen the markets gyrate, crash, boom and bust and do it all over again and again. If that's the worse they can do then my advice is to simply ignore the markets, ignore the noise generated by a media often struggling to cope with adding any real news and allow time to do what it has always done. Allow your daffodils to grow safe in the knowledge that grow they will and that time is the ingredient necessary to make the seemingly impossible, possible, as it has always done.

Weren't we told the last 106 years were the worst ever? Wasn't the Great Depression the worst ever? What about 1937 war scare crash when the Dow lost 49.1%. Wasn't that bad? What about the '87 crash in Australia? What about the 1973/5 credit crisis, which I might add bears particular similarity to the current situation. Still the share market has performed. Are you starting to see what a wonderfully predictable, stable, safe and reliable system the share market is? No?

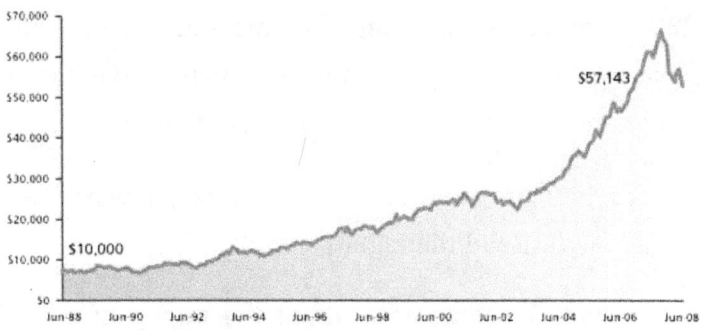

Figure #2. (Colonial First State, 2008)

The Australian market crash of 1987 provides a great example of what not to do. This infamous crash had a devastating effect on some investors while for other long term investors it had little impact. Richard invested $10,000 in a fund in September 1987. The Australian share market suffered its crash, for those who don't know, in October of that same year. After three years Richard decided to 'cut his losses' and run, thinking the market would never regain the lost ground. Richard's time in the market, limited as it was, returned a very disappointing result. An annualized loss over the three years of -10.36% pa.

Lara, on the other hand, invested $10,000 at the same time as Richard and in exactly the same fund. Lara, unlike Richard then went and sat in the North Pole for the next twenty years ignoring the world's news. When she returned to Australia to retire in

2007 (Figure #2) she was very pleased indeed with her share market's performance which delivered an annualized return of 8.55% pa (over 20.5 years).

Time in the market is what counts, always has, always will. Read that again.

Perhaps I should talk about the poppy crisis of 1635 or the run on the Bank of England in 1697 or for that matter the panic of 1819. In 1819 the US had been enjoying boom conditions after the War of 1812 ' The Second American Revolution', but it all came to a shuddering halt in 1818 when the Bank of the United States started to rein in its lending in order to make repayments on overseas loans which had financed the 'Louisiana Purchase'. Sound familiar? No? Well let me continue. The rush for cash caused a collapse in prices, and a brutal depression quickly followed, with staggering rates of unemployment. Funnily enough, surprise, surprise, the depression raged so fiercely that it burnt itself out and by 1823 everything was as it always had been and the long term investor who had the courage to stare the madness of the markets in the face continued on his journey of wealth creation. Feeling the predictability and security of it all yet? No?

Well, what about Vietnam, two World Wars, Boer War, Gallipoli, Korean War, Sept 11th? Were we not told these were bad years? The simple truth of the matter is market gyrations are no more news worthy than the fluctuation in my weight but the way the media portray them you would seriously think the world was about to end. Prime Ministers grand stand the issues; Reserve Bank Governors make wonderfully eloquent speeches when all that they are really doing is giving us all a free lesson in history.

A market that for those with strength of character can turn $100.00 dollars into $7.1 million dollars over 106 years should be good enough for most of us. It is certainly good enough for me.

The answer is the market has performed as it always has through every one of the above crises and for those who bought quality companies and held their positions time and time again the market delivered to those wise investors such predictable performance that makes it simply the best mechanism for the transfer of wealth known to mankind. For those of you who are still interested in buying low and selling high may I seriously suggest counseling.

According to the highly reputable and respected Russell Report "the Australian share market has performed better than any other asset class over the past 10 and 20 year periods and the Australian market is the 10th largest market by market capitalization in the world" (ASX, 2008). What more does anyone want?

Safe, predictable, reliable, secure, resilient these are the words that describe the market I know and love. These too are the words you will use in time to describe the market, make no mistake about that. However, if you lack the emotional intelligence and internal fortitude to stick to a plan in the face of global panic during which times the media represent themselves and the truth poorly then so be it. Good-bye and good luck.

So by now we will have hopefully lost all the people who believe that there is a fast way to make a buck, a sure fire plan, a short cut to wealth creation. Hopefully by now anyone who wanted to see some razzle dazzle has also thrown this book away in disgust and for those remaining, committed readers I shall continue.

Investment Time Horizon

You have heard me mention the term "time horizon" and what it means to me. Time horizon simply refers to the period of time you want to hold a particular asset. Typically people talk about short, medium and long term time horizons and I regret to say that the general consensus is that this relates to a time period of 3, 5 and 7 years. This, in my view, is totally unacceptable and for most, regrettable. In my view short, medium and long term time horizons should be set at 10, 25 and 50 years not 3, 5, and 7 years. If you are talking of a time period under 10 years then you are by definition a speculator and the market will deliver you exactly what you deserve.

My time horizon of 10, 25 and 50 years should, I believe, be adopted by all no matter what their stage of life as it makes no difference. The fact is that if you buy quality assets and hold them long term then time has no relevance. While many retirees in their 60s and 70s often say, God, in fifty years I will be dead (and sadly enough that is likely to be true) it should not mean that they change their time horizon or investment strategy as investing for the short term is a sure fire way to poverty.

Retirees need to realise that it is never too late to start being an investor. I am tired of listening to people tell me how well they are doing in tax effective superannuation when they have no concept of anything else that may exist outside that. How do you know how well you are doing when you have nothing to compare it to?

I often meet people who tell me that they invest in the share market and as one of few investors I am always very excited when I meet another investor. However, on further exploration of their statement I soon discover that they are not investors at all but rather speculators. Alas, disappointment once more. You are going to meet hundreds of people who are going to tell you thousands of things but please remember most of them have not a clue about the subject matter they speak and certainly even less interest in your life and well being. Speculators pretending to be investors are everywhere so be careful as you don't want to be led astray.

It is important to have realistic goals and time horizons as trying to buy into a market or particular shareholding and selling out of it in anything less than ten years is akin to trying to perform brain surgery with nothing more than a sledge hammer. It is simply not going to work. Time and time again a person's own greed gets them into situations they cannot manage, do not understand and unfortunately it ends up costing a lot of money. People need to take far more responsibility when it comes to managing their money if they are to build the life of their dreams.

The Importance of Two Dimensional Assets

So far so good. We have encouraged the 'flash operators' to throw my book forcefully in the bin. Mind you, we do need these people to continue their search for "The Holy Grail" of investment and wealth creation strategies as it helps with the transfer of wealth in a direction away from them (speculators) and towards us (investors).

So far we have looked at the Australian market and highlighted in simple terms what a wonderful safe and predictable way it offers us to create long term wealth and secondly, we have talked a little about time horizons and how they relate to one's purchase decision in the first place. Remember if you don't sell in down times you won't make a paper loss real. Ignore it and wait and the Daffodil Principle will take care of the rest.

We now need to progress to a topic almost as important as having a life plan and that is the importance of two dimensional assets.

I promise to keep this all very simple and easy to understand and I promise not to lose you here as this is critically important.

An asset is simply things we own. The dictionary says that an asset is a useful and desirable thing of quality or a single item of ownership having exchange value. So in brief, an asset is a house, a car, a diamond, a piece of art. Assets by definition are both income producing i.e. shares (income via dividends), rental properties (income via rent) and non income producing i.e. your house, your car etc so it is not surprising you hear 99.9% of people describe their own home as an asset where I prefer to call it what it is and that is a **liability**! Hang in there!

Liabilities as described in the dictionary are something disadvantageous, monies owed; debts or pecuniary obligations. So a liability is an item you owe money on or in simple terms an item that costs you money.

The definitions of assets and liabilities that I want you to use are as follows:

> an <u>asset</u> is an item that you own, grows in value over time and produces and income;
> and a <u>liability</u> is an item that costs you money.

So your house is then by definition a **liability**! Sorry, but it's true. I'II give you a moment.

It is now important to note that there are tax deductible liabilities and non tax deductible liabilities or good (tax deductible) and bad (non tax deductible) debt and for the record I have no problem with good debt so long as it doesn't leverage your total assets by more than 25%.

So, for example, if you own one million dollars of National Australia Bank (NAB) shares then I would have no problem with you leveraging your assets (shares are assets as they produce an income and grow over time) by taking a loan (tax deductible) up to 25% or $250,000. I would further add that this is a wise use of good debt (tax deductible) and is something that everyone should do but you must stay within the 25% limit. People who have leveraged themselves highly (anything above 25%) often lose and in this current climate there are many of them licking their wounds right now.

In short, it is critically important to the creation of all wealth that the assets you invest in are two dimensional i.e. produce income and grow as one dimensional assets equals poverty over time. FACT.

A two dimensional asset is, for example, a single (quality) share as not only will it grow over time it will also produce income via its dividends. So dividend paying shares like the above are two dimensional assets. A term deposit in the bank is not a two dimensional asset because it only pays interest and returns the original deposit i.e. no growth in capital. A rental property is also a two dimensional asset as it grows over time and produces an income via rent. That being said investing in property is another sure fire way of paving your path to poverty as property is not as tax effective an investment as investing in shares due to the system of imputation credits which I will discuss shortly and while the price of a house may rise its value sadly does not.

I realise this for some may be getting more complicated but please bear with me as it will soon become clear. For now, what is important for you to understand is that good assets, the ones we want to invest in must be two dimensional i.e. they must grow and they must produce an income. If they fail either of these rules, like term deposits, then they are not assets in which you want to invest.

It is so important that you are invested in two dimensional assets that I can't stress the point enough. When you consider inflation (the silent killer of wealth) it is no wonder people, especially pensioners, are finding it more expensive to live. Not only are prices going up but those pensioners not invested in two dimensional assets are becoming less wealthy day by day.

Two dimensional assets are assets that grow over time and produce income. All other assets have no relevance to the creation of wealth.

The Real Difference between Assets and Liabilities

We have discussed the Australian market in simple terms, we have talked a little about time horizons and how it relates to one's purchase decisions and we have discussed two dimensional assets being those that grow and produce an income. Now, I want to share with you some facts about the decisions you make in life in terms of investing in the Australian share market in quality two dimensional assets over the long term versus buying yourself and your family into yet another liability.

The true short story I am about to tell is that of Mick and Craig. Mick was a flash operator, impatient and believed he had the good old Midas touch. More importantly Mick had an unwavering belief that he would always win. Mick was by virtue, successful in the eyes of the general population as he had the flash house, car, bike, great job, the smart corporate wife and cute kids to match. Mick had it all – or did he?

Craig, on the other hand, was from the rough part of town and was lucky on a number of occasions to avoid jail time in his youth. Craig's motto is if I don't have the cash then I don't want it. Craig to this day does not own a credit card nor I might add, want one. Craig is old school, believes in saving and believes in making sure he and his family truly understand the value of all things while Mick was the exact opposite.

One day Mick was given the opportunity to invest wisely after a financial windfall but Mick decided against conservative, stable, secure, safe and boring advice preferring to play the share market as well as loading up on more liabilities than one should consume in a life time. Within one month of gorging himself on the material world Mick proclaimed with great gusto that he had worked out the share market and had a sure fire system in place to make money. In passing he also mentioned that his new car and motor bike were great and that he was loving life.

Craig on the other hand also came into a little bit of money but unlike Mick listened to my advice and bought a parcel of bank shares foregoing his desire for a new car or an overseas holiday. Craig knew instinctively that he needed to invest the money because once spent it was gone forever and Craig couldn't afford to lose a single cent.

Six months later - and may I remind you that this is a true story - Mick, in his words had effectively run into a bit of bad luck and had now lost his job, lost his house, his wife, his cars, his cute kids, his bike, all his money and sadly enough himself, while six years later, Craig still does not own a credit card and not only has his bank holdings grown but they have also provided him with valuable income along the way. How does the expression go, a fool and his money are soon parted? While sad, it is true and that if you fail to realise the value of money, money itself has an incredibly uncanny way of teaching you the lessons often taught but rarely learned.

I have told you this story for two reasons. Firstly, I believe that we all know someone like Mick yet we are often slow to learn from their mistakes. We must realise that one cannot consume so many liabilities without at some point in time regurgitating them. Secondly, Craig has an innate belief system that allows him to shun the toys and liabilities of today for the benefits in the years and decades ahead. If you are lucky enough to know someone like Mick and Craig keep them close to you as they are both great role models to have around. One for reminding you what not to do and the other to lead the way. There is little doubt that we all need to be a lot more like Craig and a lot less like Mick if we truly want to create real, long term wealth.

The other day a good friend of mine said, "*So James, when are you buying your boat?*" Well, the reality is, my wife and I are smart enough to realise that the cost of ownership and the forgone opportunity cost of not having our money invested is simply too high a price to pay.

Let me explain. Let us assume the boat of our dreams costs $1 million dollars, so, to fund our boat we need to sell some shares. Let us pretend that we now have our lovely boat which cost $1 million dollars and let us now start counting the real cost of ownership. Mooring fees at one of Sydney Harbour's marinas cost $25,000pa, annual maintenance a further $10,000 and to run her for one year over twenty weekends will cost a staggering $54,000 in fuel. So far our lovely new liability is going to cost us in the first year $89,000 in running costs but it doesn't end there.

We now have to add the opportunity cost of not having our $1 million dollars invested in the safe, predictable, reliable and secure share market earning 5% growth pa and 4% income pa, which, I might add, are conservative numbers. So, that's $89,000 in annual running costs plus another $90,000 in lost opportunity costs - but wait, there's more. The sad fact is that boats lose money so we need to factor in at the very least 5% depreciation for the first year bringing our total true cost of ownership of our $1 million dollar boat in at a staggering $229,000! That's right! The boat cost $1 million to buy and another $229,000 to simply own and use in the first year. The sad fact is that it's going to cost more in year two, three, four, five etc as your opportunity costs really start to take hold.

So, to answer my friend's question, when are we going to buy a boat? The answer is, not in this lifetime. Liabilities cost so much more than people dare to believe and the reality is they are costing you day in, day out, week in, week out, month in, month out and on and on it goes until one day you wake up and realise that there is simply not enough cash in the bank to do what you want to do.

I want to say that I am not opposed to spending money and having a bit of fun but if you want a boat, rent one. If you want a Porsche, Ferrari or Bentley hire one for the day; just whatever you do don't buy one. Let some other mug do that.

The real cost of decisions you make today, every day, have an effect on your financial health and I firmly believe that if humanity were a little less so self absorbed and a little more focused on what is really important then there would be no need for books like mine.

Liabilities keep on costing you, day after day, month after month and year after year whereas the private pleasure two dimensional assets allow together with the independence it affords far outweighs any short term thrill yet another liability can bring.

Why Retirees Get Poorer And Poorer

It's not because of the lousy pension; it's because of something far worse! Retirees become poorer and poorer because of a combination of their sheer lack of interest in all matters financial and secondly because of the silent killer, inflation, which is allowed to run rampant with their total disregard for its effects.

I do not feel sorry for retirees but rather frustration at governments past who did not ensure we were all equipped before leaving school with some basic financial knowledge. I believe if we had a little more education during our school years concerning money and how to manage it we would all be in a very different place right now. To say that I am scared at today's youths' appetite for debt is a gross understatement. To say that I am concerned for what the next ten years will deliver pensioners now aged sixty five would be accurate. Nonetheless, time will deliver both pensioner and youth the lessons they need to learn, let's just hope it is not too late for the majority.

Typically retirees roll up their money and place it in either a savings account (one dimensional asset) or some form of managed fund. Seldom do retirees buy direct shares, mainly due to three reasons. Firstly, their negative view on how long they are actually going to be around; secondly, their complete and total apathy towards the subject matter; and, finally, because of media's irresponsible portrayal of the share market. With all of this working against all of us, not only our retirees, is it any wonder confusion reigns supreme. For those of you who want out of the pensioner poverty cycle or if you are younger, the liability trap, there are some things you need to know.

Inflation. Your biggest enemy is inflation. Inflation is an economic concept which shows and measures the trend of typically increasing prices from one year to the next. Prices in general terms grow at around 3% per annum. So to put it simply, if you have a nest egg of $200,000 in a term deposit earning 5% after one year you have really only earned 2% ahead of inflation and that's before tax.

The problem of inflation is really exacerbated when people supplement their income via the use of the interest from, say, a term deposit. For example, 5% interest on a $200,000 term deposit will generate an interest payment before tax of $10,000 per annum. Now, when people use interest to supplement their income this leads to enormous problems very quickly. With the interest from deposit spent and inflation running in the background there is only ever going to be one outcome: poverty.

The reason poverty is the only outcome is because of the effect of inflation. The original deposit of $200,000 is, after the first year, now worth only $194,000. Basically at this rate our depositor is going to become more and more financially crippled as each year passes because he did not invest in two dimensional assets. Inflation is the relentless killer of wealth. Forget this fact at your peril.

Figure #3 clearly shows the performance of our fictitious depositor leaving $200,000 with the bank for a six year period. After six years not only has his income (interest) fallen from $10,000 in year 1 to $8,587 in year 6, his capital has also taken a pounding down from $200,000.00 year 1 to $166,594 in year 6. It is clear from this example that this depositor, like many, is going to find making ends meet more and more difficult. He will also find basic necessities becoming increasingly difficult to fund.

In this example our depositor has broken the golden rule which is to make sure all assets that you invest in are two dimensional which a term deposit clearly is not.

	Y1	Y2	Y3	Y4	Y5	Y6
Capital	$ 200,000	$ 194,000	$ 188,180	$ 182,535	$ 177,059	$ 171,747
Interest (5%)	$ 10,000	$ 9,700	$ 9,409	$ 9,127	$ 8,853	$ 8,587
Inflation (3%)	($ 6,000)	($ 5,820)	($ 5,645)	($ 5,476)	($ 5,312)	($ 5,152)
Capital Total	$ 204,000	$ 197,880	$ 191,944	$ 186,185	$ 180,600	$ 175,182
Interest Spent on Living	($ 10,000)	($ 9,700)	($ 9,409)	($ 9,127)	($ 8,853)	($ 8,587)
Capital Balance	$ 194,000	$ 188,180	$ 182,535	$ 177,059	$ 171,747	$ 166,594

Figure #3.

Figure #3 clearly shows you what happens to your income if you invest in a one dimensional asset like a term deposit. Basically it will go backwards. If, however, you stick to the rules and invest in quality two dimensional assets the opposite is true. In two dimensional assets, the longer you live the more secure you will become.

Now let's take the above example and run the numbers based on our depositor investing his $200,000 in the top ten Australian shares by market capitalization for the same period to see the difference in capital and income over the same period of time (Figure #4.).

	Y1	Y2	Y3	Y4	Y5	Y6
Capital Shares	$ 200,000	$ 202,000	$ 204,020	$ 206,060	$ 208,121	$ 210,202
Dividends Received (4%)	$ 8,000	$ 8,080	$ 8,161	$ 8,242	$ 8,325	$ 8,408
Capital Growth (4%)	$ 8,000	$ 8,080	$ 8,161	$ 8,242	$ 8,325	$ 8,408
Inflation (3%)	($ 6,000)	($ 6,060)	($ 6,121)	($ 6,182)	($ 6,244)	($ 6,306)
Capital Total	$ 210,000	$ 212,100	$ 214,221	$ 216,363	$ 218,527	$ 220,712
Dividends Spent on Living	($ 8,000)	($ 8,080)	($ 8,161)	($ 8,242)	($ 8,325)	($ 8,408)
Capital Balance	$ 202,000	$ 204,020	$ 206,060	$ 208,121	$ 210,202	$ 212,304

Figure #4

As you can clearly see by investing in safe, reliable, secure and predictable shares (two dimensional assets) our investor now has an income stream that over the long term actually increases in value and a capital base that stays ahead of inflation rather than an income stream that falls in value and a capital base that decreases when invested in a term deposit (one dimensional asset) as per the earlier example. The fact is our investor's capital is considerably higher at $212,304 compared with just $166,594 of our depositor's. That is a difference of $45,710 or nearly 25% in other terms. I know which asset class I would prefer to be invested in and what's more, so should you.

To defeat the biggest of challenges, inflation, you must invest in two dimensional assets as nothing else protects your long term position against the greatest threat there is to one's financial well being. Inflation is as deadly to wealth creation as cancer is to human cells. To ignore inflation and not protect against it is akin to financial suicide.

In conclusion, if you don't care about your livelihood, your retirement and your financial situation do what most do and outsource it, prepare to struggle and prepare for hard times. If, however, the chart above snaps you into action then great but remember the lessons learned so far as none may be broken if you want to succeed long term.

Which Shares To Buy

The truth of the matter is that I don't know which shares to buy, neither does my broker and nor will yours. All I do know is that the markets will perform as they have always done. I realise that this is not of much help to many so here you go: my advice, for what it is worth, is buy what makes sense and keep things simple. You and I are touched by large corporations every day and you know a lot more than you think. I might also add that you are more than qualified to make these decisions all by yourself, trust me. Read on and see what I mean.

When I wake in the morning I think to myself (who makes the bricks my house is built from?), I walk over to the shower and have a nice hot shower (who heats the water?), I brush my teeth (who makes the toothpaste?), I wash my hair (who makes the shampoo?), I get dressed and go downstairs and pour myself a bowl of cereal (who makes that?), I then make a few phone calls (who makes that possible?). I then read the paper (who owns it?), I then get in my car and drive on the most advanced freeways in the world (who makes/owns them?). I stop and get some petrol (who makes that?). My wife calls and asks that I pick up some bread and milk on the way home so I stop at one of those large supermarkets …. (getting the hang of it?).

We are all touched every minute of every day by large corporations who were around last year, the year before that and the preceding few decades before that and during that time their value was growing for their investors and they paid their investors dividends which over time have also grown. This isn't that hard.

Next rule is to always buy the parent company. I cannot preach this loudly enough never ever, ever, ever buy a subsidiary holding no matter how attractive its yield (dividend) may look. Always and I do mean always, buy the parent company over potentially a high yielding subsidiary. (The term yield is simply the dividend paid, divided by the share price expressed as a percentage).

A great example is listed in a book called "Motivated Money" by Mr Peter Thornhill, (Thornhill, 2002) who clearly shows the importance of owning the parent through his example of Westfield Holdings and Westfield Trusts. Mr Thornhill states that he and his wife invested $1,000 each with his wife buying Westfield Holdings, whilst he chose the income and yield that Westfield Trusts offered. As you can see from Figure #5 it would appear that over time his wife's holding in the parent company was the smarter move with both her income being significantly higher than his, but more impressive is the difference between the capital figures with her holding now worth $131,091 compared to his being only worth $2,500.

While the yield is an indicator of some things, for example, his yield of 6.7% is much better than his wife's yield of 1.6% most of what yield is good for can be found in the trash. I know the yield I would prefer to have.

Please remember yield is not an indicator of terribly much if the truth be known. I am constantly amused and equally frustrated by how often the term yield is wheeled out. One must realise that yield is nothing more than a percentage at a given point in time and indicates very little and has no relevance to me personally as I don't care what the yield is but prefer knowing that I have bought the parent company because I know that over time values in quality companies increase.

$1,000 invested in 1984.

	Westfield Holdings	Westfield Trusts
Dividend 1st Year	$ 61.00	$ 92.00
Yield	6.1%	9.2%
Dividend Paid 2002	$ 2,057.00	$ 168.00
Holdings Value 2002	$ 131,091.00	$ 2,500.00
Yield 2002	1.6%	6.7%

Figure #5 (Thornhill, 2002)

If you buy a share for $100.00 and it pays a $10.00 dividend it is said to have a 10% yield. If the share price falls the yield increases and if the share price increases the yield falls. The point is, share prices move daily and so do yields. If you use yield as a guide then Westfield Holdings looks very unattractive at 1.6% and we all know that is not the case. Over time as our capital increases are yield must therefore decrease. What would you prefer? A 5% yield on $100,000 or 2% on a million?

I can understand how mistakes were made between investing in Westfield Holdings versus Westfield

Trust as those who wanted income were lured like bees to honey for the fast money and the higher yield the trust offered. It's a real shame for those chasing fast money, as an investment in Westfield Holdings of $1000 when it floated would now be worth in excess of $148,000,000 (Thornhill, 2002). That's one hundred and forty eight million Australian dollars. Not bad for a boring, low yield investment.

I just want to remind the reader at this point that it is important that any shares you buy conform to our rule of two dimensional assets which means the shares you buy must pay a dividend - some don't - and it must grow.

Before moving on to tax let us recap. We have discussed the Australian market in simple terms, we have talked a little about time horizons and how they relate to one's purchase decisions and we have discussed two dimensional assets. We have talked about the real cost of those toys versus being more prudent and we have discussed how inflation can work in the background to make your wealth erode faster than just about anything. We have spoken of what shares you should consider looking at and I have highlighted the importance of buying the parent company. These rules are golden and must never, ever be broken.

So why shares? Simply because they are the safest, most predictable, secure, tax effective investment known to mankind. If the words 'safe', 'secure' and 'predictable' are not something you associate with the share market then that's because you are not an investor but rather a speculator. The simple truth is I stand here today with the market down over 51% and I couldn't care less. As a retired investor I am not concerned as I know the markets will perform as they always have and while the next year or two may be a bit rough the years ahead will undoubtedly make up for it.

Now let's talk a bit about tax. You may have heard the terms 'imputation credit' and 'franking'. Both terms are important and both have a direct effect on your net result and while this book focuses on Australia the lessons are just as relevant for the European and American markets.

"The imputation system provides the means by which Australian corporate tax entities are able to pass on, to their members, credit for income tax they have paid. The way in which they do this is by franking a distribution. Without the imputation system, income tax would be levied when income is earned by the entity and then again in the hands of the members when it is distributed to them" (Australian Tax Office (ATO), 2008). Put simply, imputation credits (also known as franking credits) are a tax offset for Australian residents who receive dividend income from an Australian-based company.

"So while a large proportion of the population benefits from imputation credits very few are aware of how the system works and how to use it to extract the maximum advantage. The logic of the imputation system – first introduced by the Keating Government in 1987 – is to avoid double taxation of company profits. Before the introduction of imputation credits a company's profit was taxed first at the appropriate corporate rate and then again in the hands of the company's shareholders at their own marginal tax rate when they received a dividend (also commonly referred to as a distribution).

Today, shareholders receive a cash dividend along with franking credits (equal to the amount of tax paid by the company on its profit) which are then used to offset income tax payable on an individual's annual tax return. It is important to note that on the tax return the full dividend (called the 'grossed-up dividend' and which equals the cash received plus the franking credits) must be declared as income with the franking credits used as a tax offset.

Because the corporate tax rate in Australia is 30 per cent, the maximum imputation credit attached to a dividend will be 30 per cent of the grossed-up dividend. If a dividend has an attached franking credit at the 30 per cent company tax rate it is referred to as 'fully franked'. Sometimes, depending on how much tax a particular company has paid on its profits, the 'franking rate' will fall below the 30 per cent mark and investors will only receive a partially franked dividend.

Assuming investors have received a fully franked dividend, however, if their marginal tax rate is at 30 per cent or below, the net effect of the imputation system is that they would have received tax-free income equal to the full distribution (cash dividend plus franking credits).

Even better news for those whose marginal tax rate is below 30 per cent is that imputation credits in excess of income tax liability can be refunded in cash by the Australian Tax Office. This extremely useful feature of franking credits can be taken advantage of by individuals as well as complying superannuation funds, including self-managed (or DIY) super funds. Given that super funds pay only 15 per cent tax on income, imputation credits can certainly add substance to any retirement dream" (ASX, 2008).

Imputation credits are simply a way to ensure that when you, the investor receives a dividend that you do not pay tax on that dividend which has already been taxed. So, for example if company ABCD makes a gross profit of $100.00 it would be required to pay tax on those profits at the Australian corporate tax rate of 30% ($30.00) making the net profit (tax paid) for ABCD company $70.00. If ABCD company decides to pay you, it's only shareholder, 50% of its net profit as a dividend then you would receive $35.00 (i.e. 50% of the $70.00 net profit). As the $35.00 has already been taxed at the corporate level of 30% the imputation system simply makes sure you only pay the difference between what your tax rate is if more than 30% or receive a credit if below 30%.

Australian Personal Tax Rates 2008-09.

Taxable income	Tax on this income
$0 – $6,000	Nil
$6,001 – $34,000	15c for each $1 over $6,000
$34,001 – $80,000	$4,200 plus 30c for each $1 over $34,000
$80,001 – $180,000	$18,000 plus 40c for each $1 over $80,000
$180,001 and over	$58,000 plus 45c for each $1 over $180,000

Now, let's assume you want to invest $50,000.00 and have decided to look at investing in either shares or a term deposit, with the term deposit offering interest of 5% and shares offering a yield of 4%. Most would suggest that the term deposit is the better investment choice when in fact this could not be further from the truth.

Tax plays a critical part in all investment decisions and must be understood and considered before making any decision. Without considering tax in any financial decision is like trying to ride a bicycle without wheels, it just doesn't work. Let us take a look at how these two investment decisions would effect your net (tax paid) result.

Initial Investment	$ 50,000.00		$	50,000.00
	Shares (4%)			**Term Deposit (5%)**
Dividend Income	$ 2,000.00	Interest Income	$	2,500.00
Plus Imputation tax credit	$ 857.14			
Total Assessable Income	$ 2,857.14	Total Assessable Income	$	2,500.00
Less Tax (40%)	($ 1,142.86)	Less Tax (40%)	($	1,000.00)
Add back imputation credit	$ 857.14			
Net Tax Payable/ Refund	$ 285.71	Net Tax Payable/ Refund	$	1,000.00
Gross Income	$ 2,000.00	Gross Income	$	2,500.00
Net Tax Payable	($ 285.71)	Net Tax Payable	($	1,000.00)
Net Income	**$ 1,714.29**	**Net Income**	**$**	**1,500.00**

** Excluding Medicare levy 1.5%, \
** Normalized to 5% Difference is $2,142.86 vs. $1,500.00, assumes income above $80k pa

Figure #6

As you can see (Figure #6) by investing in shares (leaving capital values out) your net result after the first year is markedly more than if you had invested in a term deposit. In other terms your net income result is almost 15% better off by investing in tax effective shares than if you had invested in a term deposit.

15% better off yet every day more and more people continue to use term deposits and think to themselves how clever they are. Compared to a garden snail I agree they are clever but compared to a real investor they are merely contributing to the investor's wealth. After all, investors probably own shares in the bank in which they have their term deposit.

Do banks offer interest on term deposits to go out of business? No, of course they don't. They offer consumers interest on their money because the banks can make more money by using the consumers' capital elsewhere. Banks use term deposit funds typically generating better returns for, guess who? That's right, for their investors. If you are happy with mediocrity then may I suggest you put your money into a term deposit and thank you for adding to my wealth as an investor in banks.

Hopefully this is all starting to make sense and things are progressively falling into place. The reality is that tax is a critical element in investing and in understanding the effect tax has can make a huge difference to your return over the years.

Why Everyone's An Expert

Expert. Nothing could be further from the truth. I have worked in four countries, visited fifty more and I have come across in my time countless clever people and yet there are only two people whom I would ever listen to when it came to investing and would only ever act on one of those two people's advice. So the dilemma we all face is, whom do we trust? Whom should we believe?

I am not so sure I have the answer to this dilemma but rather can only offer the following anecdotal evidence for you to hopefully confirm that you can't really trust anyone when it comes to getting solid, honest, forthright, conservative advice.

At an analyst meeting in Los Angeles in 2006 I sat along side the CEO and CFO on stage, wired for sound in front of three hundred young, eager, mainly American analysts whose job it was to know more about our business than we did. More importantly they were there to write buy, sell and hold reports for their company's brokers who could then advise their so-called investors (you).

What we all need to understand is that these analysts were the best and brightest America had to offer. These guys were all college educated and were at the cutting edge of their game, yet they knew nothing of our business and nothing of our financial results. At the end of the day, they provided nothing more than meaningless commentary rather than adding anything of any real value or substance.

Why is this so important? It's important because it clearly highlights that these analysts had no idea yet it is these guys that are giving your brokers information on what their clients should be buying, selling and/or holding. It is these guys who write investment reports that you may read from time to time and, God forbid, actually pay for. The reality is that there were a handful of people who knew our earnings pre announcement and none of these people worked outside the company. The idea that analysts have some inside track is ridiculous. The idea that they can forecast a company's results is equally ludicrous. The fact is that only a handful of people know a company's results and a company's financial health and unless you are in the top four or five in any given organisation you will never know and to pretend you do is, in my view, criminal.

Even Alan Greenspan (former US Federal Reserve Chairman) has been facing a firing line of questions from US lawmakers since the latest credit crisis to engulf common sense. Alan Greenspan, was once considered the infallible maestro of western financial systems but, shock, horror, he has now admitted "he had made a mistake in trusting that free markets could regulate themselves without government oversight" (Grynbaum, 2008).

Grunenthal's incredibly safe drug, Thalidomide (Distavel) proves that rapacious greed to bring a wonder drug to market before it was properly tested was alive and well. What did the Thalidomide advertisements say? "Distavel can be given with complete safety to pregnant women and nursing mothers without adverse effect on mother or child…." (Weir, 2005). Completely safe? Thalidomide? Hardly. Thalidomide was responsible for horrific birth defects in thousands upon thousands of children.

Chernobyl, Agent Orange, Maralinga, Union Carbides Bhopal, Y2K that never came Gallipoli and from Presidents to men of religion, who can we truly trust? Let us not forget President Bill Clinton who said, "I want to say one thing to the American people. I want you to listen to me. I'm going to say this again: I did not have sexual relations with that woman, Miss Lewinsky. I never told anybody to lie, not a single time; never. These allegations are false" (Lehrer, 2008). To Jimmy Swaggart, a man of religion and who was one of the world's greatest evangelistic preachers until he was caught with a prostitute. Swaggart's hypocrisy knew no bounds.

While this is all rather depressing the fact is, that we, as human beings, can be easily mislead. As such, it is critical that we plan carefully and choose our mentors far more wisely than we currently do. We must all look to the past and learn the lessons history has to teach if we are to truly succeed and avoid the trappings of the material world we find ourselves.

Where this leaves you is basically on your own but that is better than listening to anyone else, trust me! Brokerage firms make money from having you, their client, buy into and sell out of positions and then down the track buy back into those positions all over again. I challenge you to pick any large company in the world, now pick a large investment house, now look at how many times the investment house recommended to their investors to buy, sell, hold, buy, sell hold, buy, sell, hold etc.

They (your broker's company) make money when you sell and when you buy so regardless of what you or the market is doing they make money - and make no mistake; you are the one paying for it.

The bottom line is simply this; listen to yourself, trust yourself and trust the market to do what it always has. If you are new to investing or simply too scared to take the plunge on your own you could do a lot worse than investing in the top twenty by market capitalization and while I am not licensed to give this advice, nor does the above act as advice, it would be something certainly worth looking into.

Other companies worth looking at while you are at it are the Listed Investment Companies. A clever man once said *"James, this is where the smart money goes"*. Companies I am referring to are Australian Foundation Investment Company (AFIC), Argo Investments Limited (ARG), Choiseul Investments Limited (CHO) and Milton Corporation Limited

(MLT). These companies take positions across the top Australian business; are by nature incredibly conservative and have incredibly low fees.

Milton Corporation, for example, was incorporated way back in November 1938. Milton's full year ordinary share dividend has increased every year since 1993 and prior to this, no full year ordinary dividend has been less than the previous full year ordinary dividend.

Now, go back and read that sentence again. What more does anyone want? Surely we have now finally all found our Holy Grail. Let me tell you there are literally hundreds of these great companies in Australia and around the globe. The only problem is that they are too boring for the likes of most to ever get the attention they deserve. These kinds of companies together with the Daffodil Principle will create wealth and make the impossible, possible.

Argo Investments is another company that provides a wonderful opportunity, ten years ago, five years ago, yesterday, today, tomorrow, five years from now and one hundred years from now in my opinion. Argo's objective is "to maximize long-term secure returns to shareholders through a balance of capital and dividend growth from a diversified Australian investment portfolio" (Argo, 2008). When you invest in companies like Argo you are buying into a wealth of experience, an experienced Board of Directors and a stable management team who underpin Argo's effective surveillance of its long-term investment portfolio. The Board consists of six highly qualified Directors, one of whom is an Executive Director. In sixty-two years of operation, Argo has only had two Chief Executives. Words like stable, safe, steady, secure should come to mind.

Argo Investments Limited was established in 1946 and now has a market capitalisation as at 30 June, 2008 of $4.1 billion. Argo offers the novice investor a professionally managed entry to the share market at an incredibly low price. Argo's investment policy is simple. Rather than try to get spectacular rewards in the short-term from high-risk stocks, Argo's management aims to provide safe and steady growth. There are those words again!

Choiseul Investments Limited, for example, has increased it's dividends paid to it's shareholders 2.8 times in the last ten years. Dividends have increased from 8.8 cents per share in 1998 to 24.5 cents per share in 2008. "Traditional listed investment companies such as Choiseul do not rely on realised capital gains from their investment portfolio to generate profits to cover dividends. Therefore, they are usually able to at least maintain their dividends even when the value of the market falls" (Choiseul, 2008). Read that sentence again and again. I can not make it any easier.

So to recap:

- we have discussed creating a life plan as without that there is nothing else;
- we have talked about the Australian market and how safe it is over time;
- we have talked about time horizons and how important it is to be an investor not speculator;
- we have discussed two dimensional assets and the importance of getting both growth and income;
- we have talked about the real cost of expensive toys versus being more prudent;
- we have talked about inflation and how it works in the background eroding your net worth;

- we have spoken about what shares to buy and who not to listen to and, finally;
- we have talked about the net effect of tax and how important tax is in the decision to make any investment.

I hope that this is now starting to make sense and inspiring you to have the confidence to take on the market, look adversity in the face and hold all your positions both through the good and the bad times.

When Should One Start Investing

I believe from about the age of six all children should be introduced to the concepts of money, pocket money and investing and understand the concepts of growth, time, income, tax and how they interact. I am pleased to say that my eight year old daughter has shares in Microsoft which she bought herself (she saved for simply ages). Not only is she usually the first to ask when her dividends are due, she is also the first to comment on how nice it is to get them when they arrive. While I don't hold Microsoft shares my daughter does. Her reason for this is predominately because of an Xbox 360 game called "Kameo" which she loves. No more thought than that in her selection criteria which really shows you how easy it can be.

Another friend of mine buys shares regularly for his children and he allows them total control and final say in the selection process of those shares. Companies like Disney, Microsoft, Mattel, Telstra, Woolworths, National Australia Bank and Cadbury all feature. Again, you could do a lot worse.

The question of when to start investing is an easy one. Yesterday. Every day, every minute, every moment that passes is a moment in time you are not enjoying the safety, predictability and security the market delivers over time. Every moment you are not in the market is a moment in time you are exposed to other far more serious dangers and temptations that do not care about your wealth creation or life plan.

The question of when to start is easy. Start now, don't delay and trust yourself to do the right thing.

Bringing It All Together

People like rules they can stick to so in the spirit of doing all I can to improve your life I have digested this entire book into convenient bite size parcels of information that can be easily consumed. While I must confess to being against downsizing the information contained in this book the reality is that if it helps just one person then my pride will recover.

Following are the seven golden rules to wealth you need to remember. It is worth mentioning that there is only one rule that is more important than all others and that is Rule #1. All other rules are equally important and breaking any rule is simply not an option if you want to succeed and reach your goals.

Rule #1

Create a Life Plan. Without a life plan you can not possibly understand what is important and what is not. The temptations to buy that new car, microwave oven or flat screen TV will be too great. Without a plan you have no way of measuring your success or knowing exactly where you are going or more importantly how you are going to get there.

> *I have been fortunate that I have always had written goals and as such I have always had an overall guiding principle and/or principles which helped direct my life when life threw up its little challenges.*

Rule #2

Invest in the Share Market. There is little doubt that even with all the ups and downs that the share market delivers the best returns on a net basis over the long term. This is a fact.

> *I have invested in the Australian market for a long time. My love affair with its predictability is something else but the market, my market has never and will*

*never let me down and I have no doubt
that over time it will never let you down.*

Rule #3

Increase Your Investment Time Horizon. As
mentioned earlier my time horizon of 10, 25 and
50 years should be yours. It is ridiculous to expect
things to happen quickly. Real investors understand
that things take time just as with planting daffodils,
amazing things can happen when you allow time
to do what it has always done. If you are trying to
'time' your entry into, or exit from an investment,
just remember it's time in the market not timing the
market that counts.

The world is forever cutting things down, out,
making things smaller, shorter, faster and with that
people's timelines have also been trimmed. We would
all like to make a million dollars in five minutes but
that's not going to happen. Without realistic timelines
you will not, can not succeed. If 10, 25 and 50 years
is too long for you then continue doing what you
have been doing as you will have plenty of time to
regret it. Short term thinking has ruined many a
retirement.

As I have always been a planner I have no issue with the concept of sowing the seeds today to reap the rewards tomorrow as such 25, 50, 5000 years does not scare me and nor should it you.

Rule #4

<u>Only Buy Two Dimensional Assets</u>. For an asset to be worthy of investment it must have two characteristics; it must grow and it must produce an income. Without either of these two traits your plan is dead. If you ignore this rule then it will be at your peril.

As a self-funded retiree I can tell you that without the two dimensional effect of the assets I hold I would not be able to retire with a young family in total security and comfort. I would not be able to stare the global credit crunch in the face and laugh.

Rule #5

<u>Don't Forget Inflation is the Silent Killer</u>. Many a good man has be bought down by inflation and yet

this most insidious of things still plays havoc with peoples' wealth creation strategies and like most things, by the time you realise what it is, its too late. Inflation typically runs at around 3% so just to stand still you need an asset that will deliver this on a net basis. It doesn't take long to go backwards and to ignore inflation is akin to putting a loaded gun to your head and pulling the trigger.

> *For me inflation was something always understood but I realise that for some this is a new concept so I beg you to make sure you understand what it is and its impact on your investment decisions.*

Rule #6

Buy the Parent. Always buy the parent company and never be tempted to buy downstream even if the yield is much more attractive.

> *The Westfield scenario is not in isolation. Never ever be tempted by higher yields, always buy the parent company.*

Rule #7

<u>Understand Tax</u>. Tax is not that hard to work out and with the imputation credit system we enjoy you would be hard pressed to find a better investment vehicle. Imputation credits reduce your tax in a very real way meaning that your net return is larger than other forms of investments that return the same gross dollars.

> *Make no mistake we all live on net dollars and when it comes to paying the bills I know what I prefer to have in the bank.*

In Closing

The issues that confront us in today's ever changing world are vast and varied. Whether you live in New York, London, Dubai, Switzerland or Australia the rules of investing do not change, only the variables. As people we need to ensure we are constantly challenging our own assumptions and beliefs if we are to add real value to the relationships we have, the employers we work for and to ensure we reach our life goals and ambitions. Ask a few of my school buddies and I bet not many would have predicted my outcome.

The reason I have selected a range of topics within this book is that life and financial goals are simply not a single subject that can be discussed in isolation. Throughout this book the inter-relationship of subject matter is evident which in truth, mirrors real life. My greatest hope is that in future, financial planners, brokers and the broader financial industry will ask clients for their life plans before giving advice that usually runs counter. Without a plan how do they know, how do you know, how does your spouse, partner or lover know where it is you want to go?

Plan to succeed and succeed you shall.

Fail to plan and you have planned to do just that. Fail.

What I have learned through my own research and through my executive posts is that much greater understanding of life is still required. Greater understanding of what drives individuals is required before companies seek to give financial advice to an often financially uneducated public. My experience has also shown me the harsher elements of human nature and reinforced that at the end of the day, you cannot rely on anyone but yourself because at the end of the day everyone is selling something. Make sure you are in control of your own financial future.

The share market has provided my wife and I, with the choice of retirement which has enabled me to spend time with my children that I never could before. If you asked me a few years ago where my children's schools were, I would have had to say sorry, don't know or worse still, ask my PA. My daughters no longer believe I live on aeroplanes or at airports and, in fact, they now think it is perfectly normal that I am always home. Now that's worth more than gold!

History is a great teacher and is strewn with mistakes, many of which were made by well intentioned people who were in the main, clever, bright and seemingly intelligent but who simply made the wrong decisions. Learn from the lessons history has to teach and make time for your future without delay as those who can't remember the past are condemned to repeat it.

I hope that this book relates to you and the issues you face daily. I hope that by me interweaving my own experiences of certain situations honestly that it helps bring clarity and helps crystallize the issues being discussed.

Hail the long term investor!

List Of References

Argo Investments Limited [Online], Available <http://www. argoinvestments.com.au/> [23 October 2008].

ASX, [Online], Australian Share Price Movements, Available; < http://www.asx.com.au/products/pdf/share_price_ movements.pdf> [22 October 2008].

ASX, [Online], High-yield times: why franking credits multiply dividends, Available; <http://www.asx. com.au/resources/newsletters/investor_update/20050614_ dividendimputation.htm>. [27 October 2008].

ASX, [Online], Russell Report Long Term Investing, Available; http://www.asx.com.au/about/pdf/asx_russell_long_ term_investing _report_2007.pdf. [29 October 2008].

ATO, [Online], Available; <http://ato.gov.au/businesses/ content.asp?doc=/Content/24066.htm> [September 17 2008].

Choiseul Investments Limited. (2008). 98th Annual General Meeting, Chairman's Address. 8th October 2008.

Colonial First State [Online], Plan For The Long Term, Available; <http://www.colonialfirststate.com.au/producteducation/marketupdate /rule4.aspx?menutabtype=pe>. [June, 19 2008].

CNN, [Online], World's Oldest Person Dies At 122, Available; <http://www.cnn.com/WORLD/9708 /04/obit. oldest/>. [February 21, 2004].

Fox, J. (2000). How to Become CEO. Treat Your Family as Your Number One Client, pp. 138-139.

Grynbaum, M [Online], Flaws in the Free Market, Available; <http://business.smh.com.au/ business/flaws-in-the-freemarket-glass-20081024-5877.html>. [October 25 2008].

Lehrer, J. [Online] I Did Not Have Sexual Relations with That Women , Available; <http://en.wikipedia.org/wiki/I_did_not_have_sexual_relations_with_that_woman>. [April 11 2008].

Thornhill, P. (2002). Motivated Money, pp.96.

Walsh, T. (2004). Eyes Wide Open. [Online], Available; <http://fulllifeonline.com/ezine.htm#Eyes%20Wide%20Open>. [16 February 2004].

Weir,S. (2005). History's Worse Decisions and The People Who Made Them. Sydney, Murdoch Books.

WOW. [Online], Available; <http://www.wowzone.com/pampo.htm>. [February 17, 2004].

Order Form

Order, *How To Gain Real Financial Independence: The Seven Golden Rules To Wealth* book, *Life Plan Template* or *Life Plan Review* please use this order form or feel free to order online at www.drjamesellingford.com.

How To Gain Real Financial Independence: The Seven Golden Rules To Wealth (the book) Price US $14.95, AUD $22.95, GBP 9.95, Euro 11.95

Life Plan Template Price US$9.95, AUD $14.95, GBP 6.95, Euro 7.95

Life Plan Review Price US $99.95, AUD $149.95, GBP 69.95, Euro 79.95

All cheques and money orders are to be in AUD$ (Australian Dollars) and made payable to Dr James Ellingford. Postage will be charged at AUD$6.95 flat fee for up to ten copies of the book ordered, worldwide. If greater than ten copies ordered I will contact you via email to discuss the postage fee.

Please mail all orders to:

Dr James Ellingford
PO Box 3464
Dural NSW 2158
AUSTRALIA

PLEASE PRINT CLEARLY

Name: _____

Phone: _____

Email Address: _____

Items required: _____ Cost _____

Number of items: _____ Cost _____

Postage & Handling ___ + AUD $6.95 = AUD $_____

Cheque/money order total in AUD$ _____

DELIVERY DETAILS

Name/Company: _____

Address: _____

City/Suburb: _____

State: _____

Postcode/Zip Code _____

Country: _____